YOUR LAND
AND
MY LAND
AFRICA

We Visit

LIBYA

Claire

O'Neal

Mitchell Lane
PUBLISHERS
P.O. Box 196
Hockessin, Delaware 19707

YOUR LAND
AND
MY LAND
AFRICA

Egypt
Ethiopia
Ghana
Kenya
Libya
Madagascar
Morocco
Nigeria
Rwanda
South Africa

YOUR LAND AND MY LAND
AFRICA

We Visit

LIBYA

Mitchell Lane

PUBLISHERS

Printing   1   2   3   4   5   6   7   8   9

Library of Congress Cataloging-in-Publication Data
O'Neal, Claire.
We visit Libya / by Claire O'Neal.
    p. cm.—(Your land and my land. Africa)
Includes bibliographical references and index.
ISBN 978-1-61228-310-4 (library bound)
1. Libya—Juvenile literature. I. Title. II. Series: Your land and my land (Mitchell Lane Publishers). Africa.
DT215.O64 2013
961.2—dc23
                                                                2012041972

eBook ISBN: 9781612283845

PUBLISHER'S NOTE: This story is based on the author's extensive research, which she believes to be accurate. Documentation of this research is on page 60.

The internet sites referenced herein were active as of the publication date. Due to the fleeting nature of some websites, we cannot guarantee they will all be active when you are reading this book.

PLB

Contents

Introduction

From the Atlantic to the Indian Ocean, from the Mediterranean Sea to the Cape of Good Hope, Africa holds a world of variety. Africa is the second-largest continent on earth, both in size and population. Rich rainforests in Africa's central west give way to the world's largest desert, the Sahara, in the north. Small mountain ranges such as the Atlas Mountains in the north, as well as dormant volcanoes like Africa's highest peak, Mount Kilimanjaro, rise high above the mostly flat landscape. Plate tectonics literally pull the continent apart in the Eastern Rift Valley, creating deep lakes such as Lake Victoria. Human beings as a species arose from this valley about 200,000 years ago, migrating out of Africa to populate the rest of the world as early as 125,000 years ago.[1] Their descendants today split Africa's one billion people into countless numbers of ethnic groups that speak more than 2,000 different languages.

News from Africa paints a picture of a struggling continent. Of Africa's 57 countries, 33 were flagged by the United Nations as the world's poorest.[2] Africa's modern problems stem largely from the 16th century, when European powers carved Africa into colonies. Britain,

Libyan Desert

France, the Netherlands, and Italy had little regard for the traditional tribal or community borders of the African people. When colonies claimed their independence in the 20th century, national pride quickly gave way to weak and corrupt governments. Many African dictators inspired fear and caused bloodshed while squandering precious resources to create the widespread and shocking violence, poverty, disease, and famine that make headlines today.

Libya is found in North Africa, a region isolated from the rest of the continent by the Sahara Desert. Where sub-Saharan Africa is a riotous clash of color, culture, ecosystem, and wildlife, North Africa is ruled by three major forces – the Sahara Desert, the Mediterranean Sea, and Islam. Strategically located at the heart of North Africa, Libya boasts beautiful beaches, historic ports, and, nestled beneath the vast sands of the Libyan Desert, the largest oil reserves in Africa.

Ancient Greeks settled the coast of Libya in 631 BCE, founding a colony known as Cyrene. These ruins at Marsa Sousa were once a temple to their god, Apollo.

Shifting Sands, Shifting People: Introduction to Libya

Twelve thousand years ago, tribes of hunters roamed a vast, fertile plain in North Africa. Food was plentiful in this lush land where cattle, gazelles, even giraffes and ostriches grazed. These first African societies lounged in their cave dwellings at night, bellies full, telling fireside stories and painting pictures of their hunting adventures.

But around 7,000 years ago, the Mediterranean Sea shrank away from this plain's northern coast, and earth's changing winds blew the rains away. Slowly, the rich, green land dried up, replaced by brown, dead desert. Some tribesmen followed their game south, peopling the heart of Africa. Others migrated east to the Nile River Valley, becoming the ancestors of the great civilization of ancient Egypt.[1] Still others stayed, changing their lifestyle to fit the new, drier surroundings. Guided by memory, these desert nomads roamed from one oasis in the Libyan Desert to the next, seeking water and food for their animals. They became skilled businesspeople, their camel caravans ferrying goods between the Mediterranean Sea and sub-Saharan Africa across the harsh sand seas. These independent tribes became the Berbers, the ancestors of nearly all modern Libyans.

Except for trade, the Berbers largely kept to themselves, isolated by the desert. Meanwhile, foreign nations – from ancient Greece to World War II's Axis Powers – rose and fell along Libya's thin green coastline. Each conquest brought the same routine. The foreign power of the day would establish large cities on the coast, building centers of trade and culture where they could enjoy Libya's beautiful seaside climate. Native

Libyans from the desert interior enjoyed a prosperous trade relationship with the invaders in return. But each foreign power would eventually wage war and fade away, replaced by their conquerers. Through the generations, desert-dwelling Libyans have learned to only put their trust in local clan leaders, seeing that governments and their laws never last.

Western and eastern Libyans led separate lives in history's books until the beginning of the common era (CE). Natural features neatly divided the country into three provinces. Tripolitania in the northwest stretched only as far south as the coastal plain allowed. Where the Libyan Desert got too rough, the desert-dominated territory of Fezzan took over. To Tripolitania's east, the impassable Sirte Desert created another boundary. The province of Cyrenaica arose to the Sirte Desert's east, first along the coast and later encompassing the desert below it.

Citrus trees flourish in Tripolitania's abundant sunshine. Gardens along Libya's fertile coast also grow olives, dates, and pomegranates.

Even today, eastern Libyans in Cyrenaica identify more with Egypt and the Middle East, known as the *Mashriq.* Western Libyans in Tripolitania share cultural ties with countries of the northwest African coast – modern-day Algeria, Tunisia, and Morocco – known to Arabs as the *Maghreb.*

Though Libya technically lies in Africa, its heart belongs to the Middle East, thanks to the introduction of Islam in the 7th century. But unlike many Arab nations, modern Libya is a product of its history as a traders' hub, nimble and ready to change with the times. In the capital, Tripoli, English and Italian rolls off people's tongues just as easily as Arabic, the country's official language. On the busy streets of Benghazi, university students wearing jeans and t-shirts text each other on cell phones as their elders, dressed in the traditional *farashiya* white robe, meet for tea in the outdoor marketplace. Step into the desert, however, and step into another world. The Libyan Desert is one of the most remote places on earth, with few roads, few cities, and few people. Here, the old ways must stay. The Tuareg "Blue Men of the Desert" that still shepherd

Unlike some Middle Eastern countries with a traditional dress code, Libya's laws allow its people to wear modern clothes.

The hand-dyed scarf worn by Tuareg men provides protection from the sun and sand of the desert.

their flocks from oasis to oasis depend on their ancient ways just to survive.

It is life in the cities, however, that drives this young country. Thirty percent of Libyans are younger than 16 years old. Most Libyans have only ever known a life controlled by their "Leader of the Revolution," Colonel Muammar Gaddafi. Libyans rose up against his oppression in a violent 2011 civil war, fueled by similar movements in neighboring nations, known as the Arab Spring. Gaddafi's death on October 20, 2011 ended his 42-year reign. Today, Libyans breathe freedom and wait patiently as their newly elected Congress crafts a new constitution, founded in democracy. But without the iron-willed control of their "Brother Leader," can bickering Libyan tribes unite to share their first taste of freedom?

FYI FACT:

The art of Libya's cave dwellers, painted or etched on rock walls, can be seen today throughout northern Africa. Sites in the Tadrart Acacus Mountains along Libya's western border – a UNESCO World Heritage Site – and Jebel Ouenat at the border of Libya, Egypt, and Sudan have been preserved by the desert's isolation and dry climate.

LIBYA FACTS AT A GLANCE

Arabian Eagle

Full Name: Libya

Languages: Arabic (official); Italian and English understood in major cities

Population: 5,613,380 (July 2012 est.)

Land Area: 679,362 square miles (1,759,540 square kilometers); slightly larger than Alaska

Capital: Tripoli

Government: Parliamentary republic

Ethnic Groups: Arab and Berber 97%; other 3% (includes Greeks, Maltese, Italians, Egyptians, Pakistanis, Turks, Indians, and Tunisians)

Religion: Sunni Muslim 97% (official); other 3%

Exports: Crude oil, petroleum products, natural gas, gypsum and cement, chemicals

Imports: Machinery, semi-finished goods, food, transport equipment, consumer products

Currency: Libyan dinar

Crops: Wheat, barley, olives, dates, cattle

Average High Temperatures: Tripoli: January 61°F (16°C), August 86°F (30°C) Sabha: June 104°F (40°C), December 62°F (17°C)

Average Annual Rainfall: Tripoli: 13.7 inches (348 millimeters); Sabha 0.3 inches (8 millimeters)

Highest Point: Bikku Bitti – 7,438 feet above sea level (2,267 meters above sea level)

Lowest Point: Sabkhat Ghuzayyil – 154 feet below sea level (47 meters below sea level)

National Anthem: "Libya, Libya, Libya"

Flag: The red, green, and black flag of Libya was originally introduced in the 1951 Kingdom of Libya. It was replaced in 1977 by an all-green flag, but was re-introduced in 2011 by the National Transitional Council, after the fall of the Gaddafi government. The red in the flag represents the blood lost fighting for Libya's freedom, the black reminds Libyans of the dark days of Italian colonialism, and the green represents Libya's agriculture. The star and crescent are the symbol of Islam, the national religion.

National Symbol: star and crescent; hawk

National Flower: Pomegranate blossom (Punica granatum)

National Bird: Arabian eagle

Source: CIA: *The World Factbook,* "Libya"

The ruins of ornate statues and grand temples in Cyrene hint at the rich culture ancient Greeks enjoyed in this "Athens of Africa."

History's sun rose over Eastern Libya and its peoples through the accounts of ancient Egyptians. Nomadic Berbers, known to Egyptians as the Lebu, invaded Egyptian border farms to plunder goods and food. Sheshonk, who was from a Berber family, ruled as Pharaoh from 943-922 BCE. His descendants, the Libyan Dynasty, controlled Egypt for two centuries.[1]

As Ancient Greece rose to power in the 7th century BCE, its crowded population looked across the Mediterranean to Libya's shores for new land. In the region now known as Cyrenaica, they founded the colony of Cyrene in 631 BCE, just a quick 250-mile sail away from their homeland. Cyrenaica's borders today reach deep into the Sahara, but the ancient Greeks were interested only in the coast, with its mild weather and plentiful rain. Rich farms supported the colony with grains, olives, apples, livestock, and especially silphium, a now-extinct herb prized in cooking and medicine.[2] Cyrene became a magnificently wealthy capital nicknamed the "Athens of Africa," with schools of philosophy, theaters, and public baths built in splendor.

Greek culture continued to thrive under the rule of Alexander the Great, who invaded Egypt in 332 BCE and claimed neighboring Cyrenaica for his empire as well. Upon Alexander's death only nine years later, control of Egypt and Cyrenaica went to his general, Ptolemy. The Ptolemies protected Cyrenaican citizens, building strong walls around important cities and giving them their first constitution. When the Ptolemy dynasty died out in 96 BCE, control of Cyrenaica passed peacefully to their allies, the Romans.

Western Libya entered world history around the 7th century BCE as a Phoenician colony. The Phoenicians were seafaring traders, originally from modern-day Israel and Palestine. They founded the cities of Oea, Leptis Magna, and Sabratha around a gentle harbor where they found three native Berber settlements. The cities became known as *Tripolis* – Greek for "three cities." Caravans brought slaves, gold, ivory, feathers, leather, and exotic animals from beyond the Sahara Desert to Tripolis, or Tripoli.[3] Phoenicians then sailed with the goods to markets throughout the Mediterranean.

By 400 BCE, the large, organized Phoenician capital of Carthage (in modern-day Tunisia) had stretched to include Tripoli. Unlike the Greeks, who viewed the Berbers as an uncivilized nuisance, Carthagin-

An artist's interpretation of the ancient port of Carthage. Its ruins today lie near the modern-day city of Tunis in Tunisia.

ian society embraced the Berber people's love of trade and battle. The famous Carthaginian general Hannibal probably led Libyan troops in his famous crossing of the mountains of Europe, on the backs of the now-extinct North African elephants native to Libya.[4] After costly defeats to Rome in the Punic Wars, Carthage passed to Roman hands by 146 BCE. The Romans used the name *Libya* for their 4,000 miles of North African coastline.

Libya blossomed under Roman care. Roman engineers built wells and dams for the wadis that drained rainwater from the highlands, turning the desert into a huge olive grove. By the 2nd century CE, the port of Tripoli was the jewel of North Africa – a center for trade and society, a peaceful setting where the talents and customs of Berber, Carthage, and Greece mingled. The modern-day ruins of Leptis Magna still stand as a reminder of the prosperity and luxury that Libya enjoyed.

The whole of Fezzan in the southwest, engulfed by the Sahara Desert, was largely unknown to western world history until Roman times. Intrepid Roman troops were the first outsiders to venture into the desert, capturing the oases of Ghadames and Germa from the native Garamantes people. The Garamantes left no written records, but archaeological evidence suggests that they ruled the Sahara's interior for over 1,000 years. It was the Garamantes who operated the famous trans-Saharan caravans, bringing valuable goods to the Phoenicians, Greeks, and Romans on Libya's coast. Traveling in chariots, they may have introduced ironworking to Stone Age Libya. Cave drawings depict the unusual long-horned cows they herded, and also trace their caravan path from Fezzan to the Niger River with inscriptions in Tifinagh, a Berber language.[5]

Garamantes society began to crumble around 400-500 CE, in parallel with civilization along Libya's coast. A massive earthquake decimated Cyrene in 365 CE, as Rome itself began to fall to infighting and invasion by the European Vandal tribes. Libyan governors watched helplessly as the Vandals crossed the Mediterranean to raid the African coast in 429 CE. The Vandals cared little about tending Rome's gar-

Vandals from eastern Europe took Roman Libya by force. They used its ports to trade throughout the Mediterranean until their defeat in 534 CE.

dens, leaving plundered Libyan cities to rot. There was little resistance in 533 CE when General Belisarius's Byzantine army marched through Libya and claimed the territory for Emperor Justinian.

Libya's future arose in 610 CE out of the mountains of Saudi Arabia, where the angel Gabriel whispered the words of the Koran to the Prophet Muhammad. Muhammad's new religion of Islam not only inspired desert tribes, but also organized them into the caliphate, a system of religious government. Arab armies blasted across the Mashriq like a desert wind, routing the lonely Byzantine outposts and shouting the name of Allah from Cyrenaica to Tripolitania by 644 CE. Despite fierce Berber resistance in Fezzan, Arabs claimed it, too, by 664 CE.[6] They settled in their conquered lands and converted locals to Islam.

FYI FACT:

The United States Navy battled Tripolitania in the Barbary Wars of 1801-1805, after President Thomas Jefferson refused to pay Yusuf Karamanli for safe passage through the Mediterranean. The US's first victory outside of American waters is immortalized in the opening lines of the US Marines' official hymn – "to the shores of Tripoli."

The caliphate's capitals in faraway Damascus (in present-day Syria) and Baghdad (in present-day Iraq) were wracked by endless struggles for power. A faction known as the Fatimids took advantage of their distraction, seizing control of North Africa from 909-1171. The Fatimids left Libya in the care of the Zirid family of Algerian Berbers from 973-1152. When the Zirids revolted, their angry Fatimid leaders sent loyal Arabian tribes known as Hilalians to oust them. As many as 200,000 Hilalian families swarmed into Libya.[7] Hilalian men took Berber wives, creating the mix of Arab and Berber families that form the heritage of nearly all of modern Libya. As they settled, Hilalians destroyed Libya's carefully-tended crops, turning the arable land into pasture for their sheep and cattle. When the Ottoman Empire stretched to encompass coastal Libya in 1551, they made no attempt to help the agriculture there recover.

Without farms to feed their economy, Libyans turned to the sea – not as fishermen, but as pirates. From the 15th century, trade ships on the Mediterranean faced two choices as they sailed the Berber, or Barbary Coast. They could pay Libyan pirates a tribute to leave the ships alone, or face death and plunder. Pirates became vital to Libya's economy, bringing resources into port cities like Tripoli. In the early 18th century, Ottoman chief of cavalry Ahmed Karamanli formed a notoriously wealthy dynasty whose navy openly operated as pirates. The Karamanlis used their power to develop and unite Tripolitania, Cyrenaica, and Fezzan for the first time.

As the Ottoman Empire dwindled in the early 20th century, Italy saw an opportunity to join the ranks of other European powers with African colonies. Italy declared war on Ottoman North Africa in September 1911 and met with a quick Turkish surrender. By 1934,

Italian troops fire cannons from a protected battery in Tripoli during the Italo-Turkish War in 1911.

Italy had begun to develop roads and public buildings in Tripolitania, Cyrenaica, and Fezzan, restoring the ancient Roman name of "Libya" to their new colony.

Italian colonists considered it their right to settle along the Libyan coast. They shoved Libyans out of their homes and into concentration camps. Libyans fought back, but were poorly equipped against Italian dictator Benito Mussolini's generals, ordered to crush any resistance. Historians estimate that over 250,000 Libyans died at the hands of their Italian caretakers. The Italians crushed the Libyans' hopes and spirits when they executed Omar al-Mukhtar, a brave leader of the Libyan rebellion, in Benghazi in 1931. As World War II scattered

WHERE IN THE WORLD IS LIBYA?

TUNISIA

Algeria

★ TRIPOLI

Misrata   Al Bayda

Benghazi

Tobruk

Ghadames

Sirte   As Sidr

Zelten Oil Field

Awjila

Adiri   **LIBYA**

Sabha

Waha Oil Field

Ubari

Murzuk

Ghat

Waw Al Kabir

Kufra

Al Jawf

EGYPT

Niger

Chad

Where in the World

Mussolini's forces, Cyrenaican spiritual leader Idris as-Senussi led the rebels to fight again, this time with Britain's help. Defeated and despised, Italian forces left Libya in February 1943. The Kingdom of Libya, led by King Idris I, officially declared its independence on December 24, 1951.

Sayyid Muhammad Idris bin Muhammad al-Mahdi as-Senussi—also known as Idris I—ruled from 1951 to 1969 as Libya's first and only king.

"Liberty, Glory, Revolution!": Government and Politics

The new Kingdom of Libya faced many challenges. Libya's unskilled people were among the poorest in the world. Libya brought in what little cash it could by exporting esparto grass, a wild-growing weed used to make paper. With most of its land unusable desert, the country depended on foreign aid to feed its people. Desperate to raise money, King Idris granted Britain and the United States rights to build military bases in Libya, an extremely unpopular decision with Libyans who had suffered at the hands of Italian soldiers.

Libya's future changed forever in June 1959 when US-based oil giant Esso discovered petroleum in the Sirte Desert. Oil flowed through Libya's first pipeline in October 1961, stretching 104 miles from the oil field in Zelten to the port of Marsa el Brega on the Mediterranean coast.[1] Overnight, impoverished Libya became flush with cash.

For many, King Idris could not bring change fast enough. Idris invited skilled workers from other countries to claim oil industry jobs, leaving uneducated Libyan herders in the cold. Though Idris built roads and modern hospitals with some of the new oil money, most wealth poured into the hands of the few who were lucky enough to be part of the new oil businesses. Young Libyans, swayed by the popular Egyptian President Nasser and his message of Arab unity, thought the conservative Idris too old and stuffy to bring Libya into the modern age.

One Libyan influenced by Nasser was a young captain, Muammar Gaddafi. On September 1, 1969, Gaddafi and a small group of army officers ousted Idris in a bloodless coup d'état welcomed throughout Libya. As Libya's new ruler, Gaddafi declared that all oil companies in Libya must give his government a majority share of their profits. He used the massive influx of cash to develop the country's infrastructure and services. Gaddafi built roads, created jobs, filled government-operated stores with cheap food and goods, and guaranteed all Libyans free, modern health care and education.

Libya's "Brother Leader" called his government the Socialist People's Libyan Arab *Jamahiriya* – a term he invented to mean "a state of the people." In this form of government, community councils were to make decisions and then report to the government. But in fact, Gaddafi operated as a power-crazed dictator. He filled the councils and the national People's Congress with yes-men who approved his pet causes. He outlawed worker's strikes, student protests, and all other political parties; he censored newspapers, TV, and radio. Anyone who seemed to oppose Gaddafi faced swift justice, which usually left the accused swinging from the end of a noose. Libya's intellectuals fled the country, fearing for their lives.

Gaddafi's scare tactics didn't end at Libya's borders. With Libya firmly under his foot, Gaddafi looked beyond his borders to gain even more power. He sought to form "the Great Islamic State of the Sahel," talking with the leaders of Egypt, Sudan, Syria, Tunisia, and Chad, about permanently merging their borders.[2] His attempts were met with scorn and isolation. Undeterred, Gaddafi shifted his interests, next

FYI FACT:

Muammar Gaddafi was born in 1942 in a Bedouin tent on the cliff-lined Mediterranean coast near Sirte, a poor Libyan village about 280 miles (450 kilometers) east of Tripoli. Throughout his reign, the eccentric Gaddafi paid honor to his roots by sleeping in a tent – though he pitched it with bulletproof fabric.

seeking to create a unified Africa. While he openly showered poor African countries with Libyan money, his army secretly tiptoed over the borders of Chad and Sudan to try to topple their governments. Meanwhile, Gaddafi's Libya supplied weapons and bombs to terrorists around the world – in Palestine, the Philippines, and the Irish Republican Army. On December 21, 1988, two Libyan secret agents smuggled a bomb onto Pan Am Flight 103. The plane exploded as it flew just over Lockerbie, Scotland, killing all 259 passengers on board and an additional 11 people on the ground. The outraged international community imposed sanctions on Libya, refusing to trade with the man Ronald Reagan called the "Mad Dog of the Middle East."

Muammar Gaddafi

In the Arab Spring of early 2011, long-oppressed Libyans saw a chance at freedom. Riots in neighboring Egypt and Tunisia toppled dictators who ruled like Gaddafi. Sparked by police killings of protestors in February 2011, Libyan rebels organized into an army. Gaddafi commanded his own forces to hunt down and exterminate the rebel "rats" without mercy. Gaddafi's educated youth documented their "Brother Leader's" reckless violence with their cell phones, posting pictures and video to Facebook and YouTube. On March 19, an outraged international community stepped in to help the rebels, bombing Gaddafi's forces with NATO airstrikes. The determined rebel force grew in strength and numbers, taking Tripoli on August 20. Gaddafi

Libyan people celebrate their
new freedom in Tripoli.

Female voters laugh and sing for joy while waiting in line to vote in the historic elections on July 7, 2012.

himself was captured and killed in his hometown of Sirte on October 20. After 42 years of oppression, Libya was free.

Today, most Libyans look toward their uncertain future with shared hope. The interim government, the National Transitional Council (NTC), held elections for Libya's new Congress on July 7, 2012. Nearly 1.8 million Libyans cast their ballots in the first free vote in 60 years. Their elected Congress then chose Mohamed Magarief as Libya's first President, who with Prime Minister Mustafa Abushagur will guide the Congress in drafting an official constitution. In the meantime, tens of thousands of former revolutionaries have laid down their weapons. Some have joined the national police force and the new Libyan National Army. However, the safety of the Libyan people, and especially foreign visitors, continues to be a concern. On September 11, 2012, militants with ties to al-Qaeda attacked a building belonging to the United States CIA in Benghazi, killing U.S. Ambassador to Libya, Christopher Stevens, and other U.S. officials. Though President Magarief denounced the attack, the violence reminds Libyans that there is much work to be done to create a Libya where people can feel safe and free.

Like people in many other cities around the world, the people of Tripoli enjoy their public beaches.

From the Shores of Tripoli to Seas of Shifting Sand: Geography

Libya is the fourth-largest country in Africa, slightly larger than the state of Alaska, at 679,362 square miles (1,759,540 square kilometers). Libya shares its longest borders and strongest cultural ties with Tunisia to the northwest, Algeria to the west, and Egypt to the east. Libyans feel African influences, too, but less strongly, filtered through the harsh Sahara via the southern borders with Niger, Chad, and Sudan.

Libya's position near the center of the Mediterranean makes its ports ideally located for trade with Europe, Asia, and beyond. Today, over 90% of Libyans live along its 1,100-mile (1,770-kilometer) coast-line. Libya's capital and largest city, Tripoli (population 2.3 million), sits in the northwest on the fertile Jifarah Plain, separated from the rest of the Tripolitanian Plateau by the low Jebel Nafusa Mountains. The Al Jebel Al Akhdar mountain rises to 1,600 feet (500 meters) in the northeast, a brilliant green backdrop to Libya's second-largest city, Benghazi (population 1.1 million). The pleasant Mediterranean climate brings hot and dry summers, with average August highs around 90°F (32°C). Wetter, mild winters rarely reach freezing, even in January.

Nearly all of Libya's history and politics centers on the thin, green coastline, making it easy to forget that the Sahara Desert claims over 90% of the country's land. One arm of the Sahara, the Sirte Desert, stretches out to touch the coast where the Gulf of Sidra buckles Libya's coastline inward. Though mostly flat, parts of the Sirte Desert form depressions that lie below sea level, including Libya's lowest point, Sabkhat Ghuzayyil, at 154 feet (47 meters) below sea level. Crossing the Sirte was a dangerous task until the Italians built a coastal highway from Benghazi to Tripoli in 1937.

South of the coast, the land rises to meet the vast dry plain of the Libyan Desert. This region of the world's largest hot desert, the Sahara, spans thousands of miles of scorched, dry wasteland. Typical daytime highs easily top 105°F (41°C) in the summer, but can at times soar above 122°F (50°C). On September 13, 1922, a meterological station at Al Aziziyah, Libya measured the hottest temperature ever recorded on Earth – 136°F (58°C). Nighttime lows can plunge below freezing. The desert's temperature extremes power a strong, sand-carrying wind, known as the *ghibli,* that threatens the coast in spring months. The hot ghibli wind raises the air temperature and buries small towns in sand in a matter of hours, though it can linger for up to four days.

The Libyan Desert is home to wonders few eyes have seen. In the Kufra District's Calanshio Sand Sea, wind-blown dunes shaped like tidal waves rise to 360 feet (110 meters) high. Over 70 percent of the Sahara Desert, however, is sandless, its surface is instead covered in salt flats, pebbled plateaus called *hamada,* or bare rock. The Tibesti Mountain Range of inactive volcanoes in the southeast juts above the desert along Libya's border with Chad. Libya's tallest peak, Bikku Bitti rises 7,438 feet (2,267 meters) here.

The Sahara's environment is too harsh to support large populations. But lush green palm groves, gazelles, and Barbary sheep thrive at oases, sites where underground water emerges at wells or springs. Small towns have also developed at long-known oases in Fezzan, such as Murzuk, Sabha, and Ubari, and at depressions in the Kufra District in southern Cyrenaica. Despite the desert's forbidding nature, the Garamantes, Berber, and Tuareg people have thrived here for thousands of years.

Thanks to the Sahara's long reach, Libya lacks any permanent sources of fresh water. Dams on wadis, or seasonal streams that carry rainwater down the highlands, provide some irrigation and well water. An average of 14 inches (35 centimeters) of rain falls on Tripoli annually, but in some years even the coast experiences drought. Gaddafi's solution to Libya's water shortage was the Great Manmade River Project, an engineering marvel so huge that Libyans call it the 8th

The Great Manmade River is the largest underground network of pipes in the world. A map of the GMR is also featured on Libya's 20 dinar note.

wonder of the world.[1] The project began in 1984 and carried a whopping $20 billion final price tag. The GMR can carry 229 million cubic feet (6.5 million cubic meters) of fresh water daily, tapped from an enormous pocket of 40,000-year-old water known as the Nubian Sandstone Aquifer. The GMR's 1,865-mile (3,000-kilometer) network of pipelines has delivered water to Benghazi since 1991, and to Tripoli since 1996. Today, cities on the coast rely on this ancient water for drinking, farming, and industry.

FYI FACT:

In ancient times, a meteor crashed into the sands of the Sahara in southeastern Libya. The impact melted the top layer of sand for miles around, creating a surface of natural glass. Libya's unusual, greenish-yellow desert glass is prized for jewelry. Egyptian Pharoah Tutankhamen's breastplate features a piece of desert glass, carved into the shape of a scarab.[2]

This oil refinery in Zawiyah, 30 miles (50 kilometers) west of Tripoli, produces 120,000 barrels of oil products daily and provides jobs to 2,300 Libyan workers.

Chapter 5

Resources and Jobs

Through most of modern history, Libya was desperately poor, remote and with few attractive resources. Its future changed forever with the discovery of oil in 1959. Today, the oil and gas industry fuels the country's economy. Libya's workforce of 1.16 million boasts one of the highest per capita incomes in continental Africa, at $14,900. Although Libyans on average enjoy a higher standard of living than most of their African neighbors, about one-third of the population lives in poverty. With 80 percent of the country's economy dependent on oil money, Libya's wealth is also its curse. Idris and Gaddafi watched their wealth rise and fall as the price of oil fluctuated on the global market. To help control prices, Libya joined OPEC, an international oil cartel, in 1962.

Libya sits atop the largest oil reserves in Africa, at 244 trillion cubic feet (6.9 trillion cubic meters). It also boasts at least 54 trillion cubic feet (1.5 trillion cubic meters) of natural gas deposits,[1] the 21st largest in the world. Libya's oil and gas industry operates through the government-run National Oil Corporation (NOC), established by Gaddafi in 1970. The NOC manages every aspect of oil and gas production, from drilling to refining, even manufacturing and laying pipelines. The NOC also grants permits to other nations to drill for Libya's oil and gas, taking a share of the profits in return. The US, Britain, Russia, China, Italy, France, and other international powers all have licenses with the Libyan government to explore and harvest oil and gas. In all, Libya's crude oil production peaked in 2008 at 1.74 million barrels per day.[2] Though the 2011 Civil War affected the industry – Libya's largest refinery, at Ras Lanuf, shut down for over a year – the violence never destroyed oil fields or refineries. Today, production is nearly at pre-revolution levels.

NOC plants additionally refine Libya's other chemical resources, such as ammonia, urea, and methanol. Libya's other mineral resources include large deposits of iron ore, salt beds in the Sahara, and construction materials such as building-quality stone and cement ingredients like gypsum and limestone. The oil, gas, and mining industries together make up 95 percent of Libyan exports.

It is important to remember that oil, and wealth, is new to Libya. Only since the 1960s has the country had enough money to build the infrastructure that citizens of developed countries take for granted, such as electricity, roads, hospitals, and schools. So few Libyans knew how to perform skilled tasks in the oil industry, or even in construction, that Gaddafi imported millions of workers from Islamic countries to fill the labor void. Even today, experts believe that anywhere from 1 to 3 million temporary workers live in Libya.[3] And though the average Libyan has the high income to afford consumer products like cars, computers, radios, and TVs, resources simply did not exist in most places to build factories to make them. Libya continues to import most of its manufactured goods from Italy, China, Turkey, Germany, and other countries.

Agriculture is Libya's second-largest industry, nearly all of which is located along the coastal plain. Small farms in Libya produce wheat, barley, olives, dates, citrus, vegetables, peanuts, soybeans, and livestock such as cattle. Large-scale agriculture is impractical in a country where only 1 percent of the land is arable. Over 75 percent of Libyans' food is imported. Historically, much of that has come from international aid, but today Libyans pay their own grocery bill using oil wealth.

Libya's young economy struggles to make room for the old ways. Only in the last generation have a large number of young people sought out education, with increasing numbers of students continuing on to college. In 2006, 30 percent of Libyans were considered unemployed.[4]

A Libyan souk

However, some of those are Bedouins, who continue to live as nomadic shepherds, and have no need for bank accounts. Libyans who cannot find jobs in the oil industry can make their living in the *souk*, or open-air market. A prominent feature of the *medinas*, or old town centers, throughout the Arab world, a souk is where Libyans go to sell their wares. Farming families bring meat and produce to sell in souks. Libyan craftsmen and women also sell traditional handmade rugs, metal works, jewelry, leather, and pottery. Tripoli's souk is especially famous for its copper crafts. Though Libya changes rapidly around them, these proud businesspeople carry on, proving that the independent traditions of their ancestors can still be successful today.

FYI FACT:

Gaddafi's wife of 30 years, Safia Farkash el-Brasai, is a businesswoman estimated to be worth over $30 billion. She owns Buraq Air, the only air service that flies Islamic pilgrims directly from Tripoli to Mecca. She and Gaddafi have ten children together, including one son from Gaddafi's first, short marriage to Fatiha al-Nuri, and two adopted children.

Sheep graze near the ruins of the ancient Greek settlement of Ptolemais, 68 miles (110 kilometers) east of Benghazi.

Chapter

6

To Be a Libyan

An overwhelming majority of Libyans – 97 percent – are descendants of the Banu Hilal Arabs who invaded and intermarried with local Berber tribes in the 11th century. Many small minorities make up the remainder of the population, including native Berbers; Mediterranean peoples such as Greeks, Italians, and Maltese; fellow Arabs from Egypt, Tunisia, or nearby Turkey; black Africans from south of the Sahara; or more far-flung peoples from Pakistan or India, brought in by Gaddafi to fill labor needs.

The Berber people make up an important cultural minority. Some Berbers continue to live a nomadic lifestyle like their ancestors, sleeping in tents at night and traveling by camel with their livestock from one oasis to the next. Historical records from Ancient Egypt, Greece, and Rome speak of the Berbers, who called themselves the *Imazighen,* or "free people." Libyans prize the Berber spirit of independence and self-reliance.

Libya has been one of the most sparsely populated regions on earth throughout human history. The enormous Sahara simply makes most of Libya uninhabitable. Before the 1960s, most Libyans lived as nomads for at least part of the year, shepherding animals like goats, sheep, and cattle and sheltering in Bedouin-style tents. Living an unpredictable existence on the edge of the desert, Libyans swore allegiance to those around them – family first, clan or community a close second. In the isolated desert of southern Libya, tribes continue to live in small communities around oases or wadis, just as they have for thousands of years.

However, many Libyans abandoned their traditional ways in the 1960s, as the sudden gush of oil money brought jobs to the cities. Today, 78 percent of Libya's 6.4 million people live in or near cities, especially Tripoli and Benghazi.[1] Most Libyans today crowd into affordable high-rise apartments, giving up their culture's love of space, freedom, and privacy for the security of a steady job.

As clans splintered apart, Libyans felt obligated to rally behind their "Brother Leader" Gaddafi as he supported Libyan citizens with expensive social programs. Before 1960, a typical Libyan was lucky to live to his or her 50th birthday. Thanks to the free, modern health care put in place by Gaddafi, today's typical Libyan man and woman live to be 75 and 80, respectively. The face of Libya suddenly became very young as infant mortality rates plummeted in the early 1980s, resulting in a population boom. Today, 30 percent of Libyans are now 15 or younger.[2] Even more are in their twenties and thirties, the first generation in Libya to benefit from a Gaddafi-provided free college education. Older Libyans saw no reason to bite Gaddafi's hand as it fed them, despite the fact that Gaddafi was widely feared. Gaddafi's downfall came instead when Libya's highly educated youth found their voice on the internet. These young people, who had never lived in a Libya without Gaddafi, could imagine a better life.

The streets of Tripoli breathe today with the quiet joy of a long-sought freedom. However, a loud minority, now free from persecution, are openly suspicious of anyone with ties to Gaddafi. Abdurrahim El-Keib was a strategic choice for interim Prime Minister because of his status as an outsider. Though born and educated in Tripoli, El-Keib taught for 20 years at the University of Alabama as an internationally-recognized expert in electrical engineering. But today some tribal chiefs in the east demand a return to the historical provinces, arguing that their old system of loose states would serve them better than a single, central government in far-away Tripoli. And some ex-rebel groups refuse to lay down their AK-47s and follow Army Chief of Staff Yousef Mangoush, who once served in Gaddafi's army. After 40 years

Mohamed el-Magariaf has been President of the General National Congress of Libya since 2012 and continues to be the leader of the National Front Party.

of suffering under Gaddafi, everyone acknowledges that trust is not built in a day. As interim Prime Minister Abdurrahim El-Keib said, "We guarantee that we are after a nation that respects human rights and does not permit abuse of human rights. But we need time."[3]

FYI FACT:

The Tuareg are a distinct culture within the Berber community. The 1.2 million Tuareg wander the Sahara freely between Libya, Algeria, Niger, and Mali. Tuareg men wear a long scarf, the *tagelmust*, as both a turban and a veil to protect their faces from sand and dust. Known as the "Blue Men of the Desert," traditional Tuareg men pound dried indigo into their scarf to dye it a deep blue, symbolizing wealth and health.

Libyan children go to school in the Abu Salim neighborhood of Tripoli.

Language and Learning

Libya's official language is Arabic, shared throughout the Islamic world as the language of the Koran. Most people in Libya know three forms of Arabic. Classical Arabic is the written language of the Koran, and is over 1,500 years old. Modern Standard Arabic is the widely used version of Arabic today, found in current Arabic literature and newspapers. TV reporters, such as those on the all-Arab TV network Al-Jazeera, speak Modern Standard Arabic. Libya's most famous author, Ibrahim al-Koni (1948-) has written over 60 books in Arabic. A Tuareg born near Ghadames, al-Koni won the Arab Novel Award in 2010 and donated his $17,000 prize money to Tuareg children.[1]

As with all languages, Arabic speakers also create their own regional dialects and accents. Libyans in Tripolitania and Fezzan in the west speak a dialect similar to their Maghreb neighbors, while the Arabic spoken in Cyrenaica sounds more like that heard in nearby Egypt. Other, ancient languages that survived the Arab invasion linger in small communities. In remote areas of Tripolitania, an estimated 184,000 Berbers speak Nafusi. Domari, an Indian-rooted language, is also known to 33,000 Libyans. Sixty-two thousand Tuareg, spread over the Sahara, speak Tamahaq. And though Libya's official language is Arabic, many of its educated people also speak English and Italian, especially in major cities.

In its height as a colony of ancient Greece, Cyrene gained fame as a world-class center of learning. Aristippus, a student of the famous Greek philosopher Socrates, opened a school in Cyrene that attracted philosophers throughout the Greek world. The famous Eratosthenes, a Greek philosopher known as the father of geography, was born in 276 BCE in Cyrene. Eratosthenes invented a system of latitude and longitude, and became the first person to calculate the circumference of the earth.

But by the time Gaddafi came to power, the learned Libya of the past was all but forgotten, buried by invasion after invasion. In the 1950s, barely one in ten Libyans could read and write. Gaddafi's own father was an uneducated goat herder who could not write well enough to make an official record of his son's birthday. His parents worked hard to afford religious and secondary school for him. Having seen the benefits of education himself, Gaddafi required all children to go to school from ages 6 to 15, funding the schools with oil money. Libyan students study Arabic, the Koran, math, social studies, and even the arts and music. Thanks to Gaddafi's policy of mandatory education through age 15, Libya's literacy rate increased to among the highest in Africa at 89 percent in 2009.[2]

The government also offers free education beyond age 15 to prepare Libya's youth for the job market. Students can choose to study at teacher-training colleges, technical schools to learn a trade or to apprentice in industry, or newer scientific research centers. Libya's universities are relatively new, but offer internationally respected degrees. The Libyan University, the first in the modern nation, was established in 1955. Most of the University became the University of Benghazi in 1973, which boasts a modern student enrollment of around 80,000. The rest of the University of Libya split off to become the University of Tripoli. Other major institutions include Omar al-Mukhtar University in Bayda and Misrata University, each of which educate tens of thousands of students each year.

Some Libyan youth choose not to pursue higher education. Many children in rural areas are needed to help run their family farms or businesses, or simply cannot find transportation to get to college in a faraway city. For many of these families, girls are expected to drop out after 15 to stay home and care for their families, or to prepare for a family of their own. Libyan adult women have lower literacy rates – 82

A Libyan farm

percent – compared to 95 percent for men, a gender difference which is common throughout traditional Islamic countries.

Before the revolution, Gaddafi's government served up six newspapers with hand-picked, heavily censored stories. But by creating a literate, well-schooled population, Gaddafi created a demand for media of all kinds, a movement that fueled the revolution. Rebels in Benghazi created Voice of Free Libya radio in the spring of 2011 to broadcast unbiased news of the revolution. The Libya TV news station, now the country's most popular, went live in March 2011. And with over 350,000 Libyans on the internet in 2010, Libya's youth knew how to share their plight with an international audience. Pictures of the violence, and even a home movie of Gaddafi's death, were taken with cell phones and posted immediately to Facebook and blogs. Newspapers in post-Civil War Libya, such as *The Tripoli Post, Brnieq,* and *Libya Herald* have utilized their new freedom with little restraint, but must work hard to gain credibility in a place where journalism training is only now becoming available.

FYI FACT:

American filmmaker Don Coscarelli Jr. (1954-) was born in Tripoli to Italian-Libyan parents. Coscarelli is best-known for *The Beastmaster* and his horror series *Phantasm*. Because of his heritage, Coscarelli is trilingual, speaking Arabic, Italian, and English.

The Tripoli Cathedral opened its doors onto Algeria Square in 1928. The Cathedral first served the Roman Catholic Italians, but Muslim Libyans restored it and converted it into a mosque in 1970.

Chapter 8

Allahu Akbar, God Is Greatest

Life in Libya is tied to Islam, the country's official state religion. Nearly all Libyans – over 97 percent – are Muslim. It is nearly impossible to understand life in Libya without understanding Islam.

Worldwide, Islam is divided into two major sects – Sunni and Shi'a – with many minor sects scattered throughout the world. Ninety-seven percent of Libyans are Sunni Muslims, as are the majority of the world's Muslims. Sunnis and Shi'as split over a bitter disagreement following Muhammad's death in 632 CE – who would be the next leader, or caliph? Sunnis determined that future caliphs should be elected from faithful, elite Muslim scholars. Shiites bitterly disagreed, insisting that leaders must be descended from the prophet Muhammad. Though this point may seem minor to outsiders, the disagreement between Sunnis and Shi'as has resulted in hostility ever since.

A third sect arose in North Africa in the 19th century. Its founder, Muhammad ibn Ali as Sanusi (1787-1859) believed in the purity of the faith and morals of early Islam. The Sanusi order of Islam is today headquartered in the oasis town of Kufra in southern Cyrenaica. Sanusi's reputation as a holy man and a well-traveled scholar throughout Algeria and Libya attracted a devoted following. That the Grand Sanusi lived locally made him almost saint-like to nomadic Berbers of Cyrenaica. King Idris I was easily accepted as Libya's first ruler because he was Sanusi's grandson.

Libya's Berbers invented the Kharijite sect of Islam, in rebellion against their 7th-century Arab conquerors. Kharijites maintain that any faithful Muslim could be a caliph, and that both Sunni and Shi'a Muslims are no better than unbelievers. Kharijites today are found in Jebel Nafusa and scattered small communities in the Muslim world.

National Transitional Council leader Mustafa Abdel Jalil announced in October 2011 that a new Libyan constitution, like those in many other Arab nations, would consider shari'a law.[1] Shari'a law is based on careful study of Islam's *sunnah,* or ways of living, spelled out in the holy book of the Koran and in the *hadith,* accounts of Muhammad's life and deeds. Many aspects of shari'a seem old fashioned or even cruel to outsiders. Countries with shari'a law often use corporal punishment carried out in public, like cutting off the hands of thieves, or death sentences for those who change their religion from Islam. However, Libyans would argue that shari'a law protects a family's honor, and encourages all citizens to be modest, honest, and fair.

Libyans observe Islam's holidays with both public and family celebrations. Islam follows a lunar calendar instead of the traditional Gregorian, solar calendar, with Arabic names for each 29- or 30-day month. Libyans celebrate New Year's Day, or *al-Hijra,* on Muharram 1. *Mawlid* celebrates the birthday of the Prophet Muhammad during the month of Rabi' al-awwal with parades, carnivals, and sharing food with the poor.

Islam's holy month is Ramadan, commemorating the time during which Allah gave the first words of the Koran to Muhammad. Each morning just before dawn, Libyans start their day with a special meal, called *suhur.* After suhur, Muslims do not eat or drink all day, until dusk signals the end of the day's fast. Traditional families eat dates first, as the Prophet did, and then break their fast with *iftar,* a meal that usually includes soup, rice and meat. Ramadan ends in *Eid al-Fitr,* a three-day celebration of parties and feasts. Eid al-Fitr symbolizes a clean start, a time when many couples marry and families buy their children new clothes and clean their houses.

Arafa is a day of repentance, commemorating the final sermon of Muhammad during the month of Dhu al-Hijjah. Many Libyans spend this day in prayer and fasting. The day after Arafa begins the four-day Feast of the Sacrifice (*Eid al-Adha*), honoring Ibrahim (known as

Mecca, holiest site in Islam

FYI FACT:

Under Gaddafi, many of Libya's Muslims lived and died without fulfilling their religious obligation to make one trip (or *hajj*) to Mecca, the birthplace of Islam. Mecca's leaders only allow 7,000 *hajj* visas to Libyans each year to control crowds. Gaddafi handed these visas to his relatives or political allies in Libya. After Gaddafi's death, the National Transitional Council facilitated free *hajj* for as many as 7,500 Libyans who had lost loved ones in the Civil War.[2]

Abraham in the Bible) for obeying God's word, even to the point of almost sacrificing his son Ishmael (or, in the Bible, Isaac). Families feast on whole roasted lamb, saving one-third of the meat to give to the poor.

Libya's government holidays are not as festive as Islamic holidays, but they are enjoyed as a day off work to spend with family. Beginning in 2012, Libyans celebrate Revolution Day on February 17, commemorating the start of the people's revolution against Gaddafi. A new national holiday, Liberation Day, is celebrated on October 23 to mark the anniversary of Libya's official announcement of freedom from Gaddafi. Deportation Day on October 26 is a national day of mourning, remembering the suffering of Libyans under the Italian occupation. Libya's independence from Italy is celebrated every year on December 24, the day the Kingdom of Libya was established.

Today, Libyan families can enjoy the streets of Benghazi. This father and daughter are attending a peaceful demonstration in support of the new government.

Family, Food, and Fun

Nothing is more important to Libyans than family. Historically, communities formed around extended families called clans. Even today, Libyans typically share their household with extended family – parents, their unmarried children, and elderly or unmarried female relatives. As in typical Islamic families, the father is considered the head of the household. Young men are often only considered adults when they marry and begin a household of their own. Today's Libyan parents have an average of three children, down from a high of seven children during the baby boom in the early 1980s. Boys are seen as special blessings, though Libyans consider it their duty to spoil and brag about all of their children.

Gaddafi's strong belief in equal rights for women set him apart from the leaders of many other conservative countries, and shaped the freedoms Libyan women enjoy today. Women in Libya have been able to vote since the early 1960s. Several women have even served in high-ranking government positions. Gaddafi passed laws guaranteeing women equal pay beginning in 1970, and even required women to register for the military starting in 1984. Libyan law protects women from being forced to marry against their will, though many marriages are still arranged by the parents of the bride and groom. Libyan women can also drive, own property, and divorce their husbands. But despite these freedoms, only 30 percent of Libyan women hold jobs. Traditional Islamic attitudes persist in this conservative country, with a cultural belief that a woman's highest calling is to protect her honor by staying home and taking care of her family.

Many other Islamic countries have strong social pressures or even laws that forbid Western-style clothing. In Yemen, women cover everything but their eyes in flowing black cloth. Women in Saudi Arabia face fines and lashings if they expose their hair in public. In contrast, Libyan dress is much more relaxed. Cities teem with both men and women in Western-style, but modest jeans and shirts. Many women may cover their hair with a matching colorful scarf. Older women or those from very conservative families may choose to wear a farashiya, a long, flowing white gown that covers from head to toe. Conservative men traditionally wear a white gown over a loose shirt and trousers, often with a tight-fitting knit cap that symbolizes their devotion to Islam.

At mealtimes, Libyans enjoy the traditional flavors of many Mediterranean cultures – dates, olives, and spicy dishes that use couscous and vegetables – shared with family and friends. A cup of tea awaits any guest; coffee is also popular. Two popular dishes include bazeen, a barley bread that is boiled in salt water, and Sharba Libiya, a thick spicy soup that is practically considered the national dish (see recipe). Meatless meals are common, but on special days, such as Fridays (the Islamic holy day) or when guests come for dinner, good manners dictate that a Libyan host must serve large helpings of lamb or mutton. Though forks and spoons are found throughout the modern restaurants of Tripoli, at home Libyans pass a common dish around the table and scoop out what they want using three fingers, or with flatbread held in the right hand. Islamic law forbids pork and alcohol.

Libyans play a variety of local instruments, such as the zokra (a type of bagpipe), the oud (a lute), or the darbuka (a goblet-shaped drum held sideways and played with the fingers). Bedouin poet-singers make their nomadic work lighter when they sing the huda, or camel-herding song. Others in Libya prefer to hear modern pop music from Benghazi's Tribute FM radio station, launched in May 2011. One of modern Arabic music's heroes, Nasser el-Mezdawi (September 5, 1950-), hails from Libya. El-Mezdawi's music combines four styles – traditional

Berber instruments, African rhythms and melodies, along with Arab and European influences – to create a new sound that has inspired many modern Arab pop musicians.

Camel and horse racing have been favorite spectator sports for thousands of years. Modern Libyans, however, especially love to play and watch football (American soccer). Their national football team, the Mediterranean Knights, was formed in 1918, and has played internationally since 1953. The Libyan team placed second in the African Cup of Nations tournament in 1982, and were runners-up in the 1964 Arab Nations Cup. In 2012, they achieved their highest rank to-date, 36th in the world, and on the rise, displaying the red, black, and green uniforms of the new Libyan flag and rallying the nation with their team spirit.

Libyans tend to prefer practical over professional art. Instead of art museums, Libyans have enjoyed Benghazi cartoonist Mohamed Zwawi's funny and often political drawings, which were published even in Gaddafi's censored newspapers. Instead of movie theaters, Libyans love to see folk dances and parades at city festivals. And Libyan craftsmen pride themselves on making

Darbuka

everyday objects into art. Handpainted pottery, jewelry, and carpets woven in bold patterns of reds and black make a trip to the souk a feast for the eyes.[1]

The Arch of Marcus Aurelius, built in 163 CE, still stands in Tripoli's medina. It is the only structure that remains from the Roman town of Oea.

Chapter 10

We Visit Libya

Libya has much to offer the world traveler – five UNESCO World Heritage Sites of ancient ruins; some of the cleanest beaches on the Mediterranean, dusted with powdery white sand; an alien desert waiting to be explored. Friendly Libyans love to show off their country. However, world travelers perceive Libya as a dangerous place, scared away by Gaddafi's reign and violence that wracked the country in 2011. Tourist revenues currently make up less than 1 percent of the country's revenue.[1] Most of Libya's 1.2 million annual visitors come from Egypt and Tunisia, hopping over Libya's border to visit family. With the new government's focus on safety and stability, perhaps the new Libya will soon be free to showcase its hidden treasures.

A journey to Libya begins and ends in Tripoli, home of the country's largest international airport. Take in Tripoli's popular beach for a dip in the Mediterranean, or just to people-watch. Or, head to the medina to take a trip back in time. Explore the Red Castle Museum, built atop a 2nd century CE Roman fort, now home to fabulous archaeological treasures. The museum boasts a four-story collection of Greek and Roman mosaics, coins, and artifacts, as well as exhibits on modern history and Libya's geology and wildlife. Sip tea at a café next to a surviving Roman relic, the almost 2,000-year-old Arch of Marcus Aurelius. Italians built the historic Martyrs' Square as a grand downtown space that marks the entrance to Tripoli's souk.

Entire ancient cities lie in spectacular ruin a short drive from Tripoli. Visit the remains of the bustling former Phoenician trading post of Sabratha 50 miles (80 kilometers) to the west. Though today this original city of the three cities of Tripolis sits abandoned by the sea, its marble columns, intricate mosaics, temples, and even a 5,000-seat theater tell of a town that was once prosperous. Or travel 75 miles (121 kilometers) east of Tripoli to see ruins of the Roman city, Leptis Magna, a favorite destination of Libyans and international tourists alike. The wealthy Emperor Septimus Severus spared no expense in decorating his hometown, hauling in granite columns from Egypt, the best sculptors from Pergamon, even marble toilet seats from Greece. Whether enjoying the sea breeze, spotting lizards scampering over the theater seats, or visiting the nearby archaeological museum, Libya's ruins themselves are a tourist's treasure.

The port of Misrata lies a 61-mile (98-kilometer) drive to the east of Leptis Magna along the Libyan Coastal Highway. Italian dictator Benito Mussolini commissioned this major road in the 1930s, which runs the length of Libya and connects Tripoli with all of Libya's coastal cities. Misrata serves as one of Libya's major business centers from its perch atop the entrance to the Gulf of Sirte. Gaddafi's hometown of Sirte, 152 miles away (245 kilometers), once bustled with oil industry activity, but was nearly decimated by the violence of the 2011 Civil War. A further 205 miles (330 kilometers) east of Sirte sits the seaport of Brega, the southern-most point of the Mediterranean Sea.

The cultural and intellectual mecca of Benghazi, 147 miles (237 kilometers) to the north of Brega, is another must-see. Inhabited since 525 BCE, Benghazi can claim standing ruins from all periods in Libya's history. The Greeks thought the area so beautiful that they chose it as their mythological Garden of the Hesperides, the site of Queen Hera's magical apple orchard. Benghazi today is a lively mix of high-rises, souks, and beaches, all framed by the emerald green of the Al Jebel Al Akhdar mountain. Benghazi may be Libya's most forward-thinking city, thanks to its popular university, and is proud to have been the birthplace of the 2011 Libyan Civil War.

Travel further east along the coast to Bayda, to visit the nearby ruins of Greek Cyrene. Unlike their Roman counterparts, these extensive ruins are lucky to be around today, having been completely

FYI FACT:

According to legend, the location of the border between Tripolitania and Cyrenaica was determined by a footrace! Runners left Carthage and Cyrene at the same time, understanding that where they met would become the official border. Carthage's runners, the Philaeni brothers, ran twice as fast as their Greek opponents. When the sore-loser Greeks accused them of cheating, the proud Philaeni brothers asked to be buried alive at the finish line to prove their innocence. Over 2000 years later, Italian dictator Mussolini commissioned a marble monument over the legendary site of their grave.

neglected by modern governments. The Temple of Zeus, the largest of its kind in Africa, dates from the 5th century BCE. Bayda also serves as the gateway to the Kufra District, 560 miles (900 kilometers) south into the Libyan Desert.

Libya's desert oases are not to be missed. These watering holes stand out as a riot of green against an otherwise unending sea of sand. Oases served an important historical role; finding these islands of water in the harsh desert meant the difference between life and death. Today, they present the easiest way for African tourists to access the Sahara Desert. Explore the mysterious history of the Garamantes people at the pyramids of Germa. From the town of Ghat in southwest Fezzan, head east with a tour guide to camp on the dunes and to see the ancient cave art of Tadrart Acacus, dating as far back as 12,000 BCE. At the western oasis town of Ghadames, see the Pearl of the Sahara – its bleached white Old City, estimated to be over 2,000 years old. Ghadames is especially popular in October, when the city hosts a grand and colorful festival showcasing Libya's folk culture and music.

Libyans are a proud people, striving to create a nation they can be proud of. But in a land older than history, today's Libya is young. Money and attention from tourism would help insulate Libya's economy from wild swings in the oil market, as well as protect its rare archaeological finds. Cautiously, visitors are beginning to return, to enjoy the wonders of this amazing country where the Mediterranean and the Sahara collide.

Sharba Libiya (Libyan Soup)

Libyans consider this thick, spicy soup as their national dish. It is served at nearly every restaurant and is a special favorite with families to break their Ramadan fast.

2 Tbsp olive oil
½ lb lamb or chicken, cubed
1 onion, chopped
2 tomatoes, diced
2 Tbsp tomato paste
1 c canned chickpeas (½ of a 15-oz can)
1 tsp turmeric
½ tsp cayenne pepper (less if you don't like spicy foods)
2 tsp paprika
½ tsp cinnamon
½ tsp cardamom
3 bay leaves
8 c water
1½ Tbsp dried parsley
½ c orzo, pearl barley, or other very small pasta
½ Tbsp dried mint
1 Tbsp fresh cilantro, chopped (optional)
Fresh flatbread
Lemon wedges

1. With adult supervision, heat oil over medium heat in a large, heavy pot. Add the lamb and onion; cook for 5 minutes, stirring frequently, until just beginning to brown.
2. Stir in the tomatoes, tomato paste, chickpeas, turmeric, cayenne, paprika, cinnamon, cardamom, and bay leaves. Add 8 cups of water. Bring to a boil, cover with a heavy lid, and reduce heat to low. Simmer for 45 minutes.
3. Use a spoon to remove the bay leaves. Add the dried parsley, and increase heat to boiling. Add orzo (or barley) and boil for 15 minutes or until the orzo is tender.
4. Remove the soup from heat. Rub the dried mint between your hands and sprinkle it into the pot. Stir to mix in the mint. Serve the soup in bowls garnished with cilantro (optional), alongside fresh bread and lemon wedges.

Adapted from Florence Fabricant, "In Libya, for Starters, It's the Soup," *The New York Times,* January 4, 2006.

Sahara Desert
Rock Art

Over 10,000 years ago, hunter-gatherer tribes depicted scenes from the Sahara in paintings and carvings on caves and other stone. This artwork has survived the test of time. Rock art has been found throughout the central Sahara, from the Aïr Mountains of Niger, through Morocco and Algeria, to Tadrart Acacus and the Tibesti Mountains in Libya, to the famous Cave of Swimmers in Egypt. The inaccessible nature of the desert kept the art a local secret until World War II.

You can create your own rock art using natural materials, just like the Paleolithic peoples of North Africa. This messy, fun craft is best enjoyed outside.

You will need:
paper
pencil
ruler
strongly colored natural materials available around your house (examples include: charcoal, white chalk, grape juice, berries, grass and/or fresh leaves of different colors, flower petals, dirt, clay, smashed terracotta pots)
bowls
spoons
paintbrush
water
large rock from your yard or a garden store, or a large, unglazed terracotta tile

1. Using the ruler and pencil, draw a grid on a sheet of paper with 8 to 10 spaces to test your palette of natural materials. Label each space with the name of one material.
2. Rub each material over its space on the paper. Charcoal, white chalk, and dirt will leave strong markings this way and can be used to color your rock just like crayons. Do the other materials make a mark?
3. Place each of your materials in separate bowls and break or tear them into pieces with your fingers or crush them well with a spoon. Add just a little water to make a paste or a thin watercolor paint. Paint each solution onto its grid space one at a time, rinsing your brush well between materials. Now you have a palette of colors with which to paint your stone.
4. Plan your rock art. Ancient stone art often depicts hunting because it was an important part of Paleolithic peoples' lives. What's important in your life? In 10,000 years, what would you want archaeologists to know about you?
5. Create your own rock art on your stone. Paint with your palette of natural pigments. Use the spoon or pencil point to carve lightly into the rock to accent your art. Leave your rock in a sheltered place to dry for several days. Or several millennia.

BCE

12,000– 8,000   Nomadic herding tribes roam Northern Africa, leaving behind their mark in rock wall art in places like the Tadrart Acacus Mountains.

1100-900   Phoenicians begin establishing colonies on Africa's Mediterranean coast.

943-730   Egypt is ruled by a Berber dynasty, beginning with Pharaoh Sheshonk I.

631   Greek immigrants found the city of Cyrene.

400s   Carthage, a former Phoenician colony, establishes major cities in Libya.

331   Alexander the Great claims Cyrenaica. Upon his death, he leaves his general, Ptolemy of Egypt in charge, beginning the Ptolemaic dynasty.

96   Ptolemaic dynasty dies out, passing control of Cyrenaica to the Romans.

CE

115-118   Jews in Cyrenaica revolt against the Romans in bloody fighting that kills as many as 200,000.

300   Roman Emperor Diocletian first uses the name "Libya."

435   Vandals from Germany raid Roman North Africa. Only Oea (now Tripoli) remains inhabited; all other cities are destroyed.

533   The Byzantine General Belisarius claims coastal cities in North Africa for the Eastern Roman Empire.

642   Cyrenaica is conquered by the Islamic caliphate. The remainder of Mahgreb North Africa follows within the next 70 years.

1551   The Ottoman Empire captures Tripoli from the Knights of St. John, extending their rule across the Mahgreb.

1711-1832   The Karamanli Dynasty of Ottoman governors controls Libya.

1911-1943   Italy controls Libya until Mussolini's defeat in World War II. Italian governors give the country its modern borders and name.

1942   Muammar Gaddafi is born.

1951   The Kingdom of Libya forms as an independent state, headed by King Idris I.

1959   Oil is discovered in Libya.

1969   The Revolutionary Command Council overthrows King Idris; Gaddafi becomes Libya's leader.

1988   Pan Am Flight 103 explodes over Lockerbie, Scotland. Evidence suggests that Gaddafi-funded terrorists planted the bomb.

2008   Italian Prime Minister Silvio Berlusconi apologizes for abuses suffered by Libyans under Italian occupation, and promises to invest $5 billion into Libya.

2011   Gaddafi's forces kill five protesters on February 17, beginning the People's Revolution against him. In March, NATO authorizes a no-fly zone over Libya to protect rebel troops from Gaddafi's air force. Rebels kill Gaddafi and his son in their hometown of Sirte on October 23.

2012   Free elections are held on July 7 to choose Libya's new Congress.

2012   September 11, 2012, Militants with ties to al-Qaeda storm a CIA Annex in Benghazi, killing U.S. Ambassador Christopher Stevens and three other Americans.

CHAPTER NOTES

Introduction
1. University Of Utah, *ScienceDaily,* "The Oldest Homo Sapiens: Fossils Push Human Emergence Back To 195,000 Years Ago," February 23, 2005.
2. United Nations OHRLLS, "Least Developed Countries," 2010.

Chapter 1. Shifting Sands, Shifting People: Introduction to Libya
1. Thomas Sheppard, UNESCO World Heritage Centre, "Workshop on the Conservation and Management of the Proposed Jebel Ouenat Protected Area (Egypt, Libya and Sudan): Technical Report," May 2004.

Chapter 2. From Lebu to Libya: History of Libya
1. John Wright, *Libya* (New York: Frederick A. Praeger, 1969), p. 30.
2. Ibid., p. 43.
3. Ibid., p. 53.
4. Philip Rance, "Hannibal, Elephants and Turrets in Suda 438 [Polybius Fr. 162B] – An Unidentified Fragment of Diodorus," *The Classical Quarterly,* vol. 59, issue 1, April 23, 2009, p. 106.
5. John Wright, *Libya* (New York: Frederick A. Praeger, 1969), p. 36.
6. Helen Chapin Metz, *Libya: a Country Study* (Washington, DC: United States Government Federal Research Division, 1989), p. 11.
7. Ibid., p. 15.

Chapter 3. "Liberty, Glory, Revolution!": Government and Politics
1. Agnes Newton Keith, *Children of Allah: Between the Sea and the Sahara* (New York: Little, Brown Books, 1966), p. 426.
2. Roger Jones, *Culture Smart! Libya* (London: Kuperard, 2008), p. 45.

Chapter 4. From the Shores of Tripoli to Seas of Shifting Sand: Geography
1. John Watkins, "Libya's thirst for 'fossil water.'" BBC World Service, March 18, 2006.
2. "Tut's Gem Hints at Space Impact," BBC News, July 19, 2006.

Chapter 5. Resources and Jobs
1. U.S. Energy Information Administration, "Libya," http://205.254.135.7/countries/country-data.cfm?fips=LY
2. "Libya's Crude Oil Production," *The Globe and Mail,* October 21, 2011.
3. David Mack, "Libya: A Country Profile," in *The Middle East,* ed. Robin Surratt (Washington, DC: Congressional Quarterly Press, 2005), p. 356.
4. Andrew Solomon, "Circle of Fire," *The New Yorker,* May 8, 2006.

Chapter 6. To Be a Libyan
1. The World Bank, "Libya," http://data.worldbank.org/country/libya.
2. Ibid.
3. William Evans, "Former Faculty Elected Prime Minister of Libya," *The Crimson White,* November 3, 2011.

Chapter 7. Language and Learning
1. Hartmut Fahndrich, "Ibrahim al-Koni," translated by Rafael Newman, Swissworld.org, Federal Department of Foreign Affairs, Switzerland.
2. The World Bank, "Libya," http://data.worldbank.org/country/libya.

Chapter 8. Allahu Akhbar, God Is Great
1. Elizabeth Tenety, "Sharia Law for Libya?," *The Washington Post,* October 24, 2011.
2. Ikram Al-Yacoub, "Libyan pilgrims enjoy hajj sans Qaddafi," *Al Arabiya News,* November 6, 2011.

Chapter 9. Family, Food, and Fun
1. James Azema, *Libya Handbook: The Travel Guide* (Bath, UK: Footprint Handbooks, 2000), p. 5.

Chapter 10. We Visit Libya
1. Elie Milky and Sophie Perret, "Tripoli, Libya – A Prosperous Prospect," 4Hoteliers, September 23, 2008.

Books

Harmon, Dan. *Libya*. Broomall, PA: Mason Crest Publishers, 2009.
Hunter, Nick. *Libya*. Chicago: Heinemann-Raintree, 2012.
Naden, Corinne J. *Muammar Qaddafi*. San Diego: Lucent, 2004.
Stolz, Joelle. *The Shadows of Ghadames*. New York: Yearling, 2006.
Willis, Terri. *Libya*. New York: Scholastic, 2008.

On the Internet

Iasevoi, Brenda. "The Fight for Libya." *Time for Kids,* August 22, 2011.
    http://www.timeforkids.com/news/fight-libya/12076
Libyana – the Culture of Libya http://www.libyana.org/
Libyan Embassy in London http://libya.embassyhomepage.com/
Sahara http://www.saharajournal.com/
Temehu, Libyan Tourism http://www.temehu.com/

Works Consulted

Al-Yacoub, Ikram. "Libyan pilgrims enjoy hajj sans Qaddafi." *Al Arabiya News,* November 6, 2011.
Azema, James. *Libya Handbook: The Travel Guide*. Bath, UK: Footprint Handbooks, 2000.
Evans, William. "Former Faculty Elected Prime Minister of Libya." *The Crimson White,* November 3, 2011.
Fabricant, Florence. "In Libya, for Starters, It's the Soup." *The New York Times,* January 4, 2006.
Fahndrich, Hartmut. "Ibrahim al-Koni." Translated by Rafael Newman. Swissworld.org, Federal Department of Foreign Affairs, Switzerland. http://www.swissworld.org/en/switzerland/resources/why_switzerland/ibrahim_al_koni/.
Jones, Roger. *Culture Smart! Libya*. London: Kuperard, 2008.
Keith, Agnes Newton. *Children of Allah: Between the Sea and the Sahara*. New York: Little, Brown Books, 1966.
Lewis, M. Paul, ed. *Ethnologue: Languages of the World*. Dallas, Tex.: SIL International, 2009.
"Libya's Crude Oil Production," *The Globe and Mail,* October 21, 2011.
"Libya Timeline." BBC News. http://www.bbc.co.uk/news/world-africa-13755445
MacFarquhar, Neil. "An Erratic Leader, Brutal and Defiant to the End." *The New York Times,* October 20, 2011.

Mack, David. "Libya: A Country Profile." in *The Middle East.* ed. Robin Surratt. Washington, DC: Congressional Quarterly Press, 2005.

Metz, Helen Chapin. *Libya: a Country Study.* Washington, DC: United States Government Federal Research Division, 1989.

Milky, Elie, and Sophie Perret. "Tripoli, Libya – A Prosperous Prospect." 4Hoteliers, September 23, 2008. http://www.4hoteliers.com/4hots_ fshw.php?mwi=3375.

Rance, Philip. "Hannibal, Elephants and Turrets in Suda 438 [Polybius Fr. 162B] – An Unidentified Fragment of Diodorus." *The Classical Quarterly,* vol. 59, issue 1, April 23, 2009, pp. 91-111.

Rogerson, Barnaby. *A Traveller's History of North Africa.* New York: Interlink Books, 1998.

Solomon, Andrew. "Circle of Fire." *The New Yorker,* May 8, 2006.

Tenety, Elizabeth. "Sharia Law for Libya?" *The Washington Post,* October 24, 2011.

The World Bank. "Libya." http://data.worldbank.org/country/libya.

"Tut's Gem Hints at Space Impact." BBC News, July 19, 2006. http:// news.bbc.co.uk/2/hi/science/nature/5196362.stm.

Sheppard, Thomas. "Workshop on the Conservation and Management of the Proposed Jebel Ouenat Protected Area (Egypt, Libya and Sudan): Technical Report." UNESCO World Heritage Centre, May 2004.

United Nations OHRLLS. "Least Developed Countries." 2010. http:// www.unohrlls.org/en/ldc/25/

United States Central Intelligence Agency. "Libya." *The World Factbook,* September 24, 2012. https://www.cia.gov/library/publications/the-world-factbook/geos/ly.html.

United States Department of State. "Background Briefing on Libya." March 8, 2012. http://www.state.gov/r/pa/prs/ps/2012/03/185461. htm.

University Of Utah. "The Oldest Homo Sapiens: Fossils Push Human Emergence Back To 195,000 Years Ago." *ScienceDaily,* February 23, 2005.

U.S. Energy Information Administration. "Libya." May 15, 2012. http://205.254.135.7/countries/country-data.cfm?fips=LY

Watkins, John. "Libya's thirst for 'fossil water.'" BBC World Service, March 18, 2006.

Wright, John. *Libya.* New York: Frederick A. Praeger, 1969.

arable (AR-uh-bull) – able to be farmed

caliph (KAY-liff) – Islamic ruler, similar to an emperor

caliphate (KAH-luh-fayt) – the government of, or lands ruled by a caliph

cartel (car-TELL) – an international alliance formed to control prices on a good or service

coup d'état (koo dey-TAH) – a swift change in the government, usually accomplished with force

depression (dee-PRESH-un) – a low point on the landscape

faction (FAK-shun) – a small group that separates itself from a larger group

fast – to purposefully refrain from eating and/or drinking

ghibli (GIB-lee) – a hot wind in the North African desert that carries dust and sand

hadith (ha-DEETH) – a collection of stories and customs about the Prophet Muhammad and his followers

hamada (HA-ma-da) – a rocky, sandless desert landscape

lunar calendar (LOO-ner KAL-uhn-der) – a yearly calendar based on the cycles of the moon; months are, on average, 29.5 days long

medina (muh-DEEN-uh) – historic downtown or city center

nomad (NOH-mad) – a wanderer; a person without a permanent home

oasis (oh-AY-sis) – a natural spring or water source in the desert

sanctions (SANK-shuns) – a punishment against a country, such as withholding trade, used to enforce an internationally accepted law

scarab (SKAR-uhb) – a gem cut in the shape of a beetle

shari'a law (shah-REE-uh law) – Islamic law based on the Koran, the hadith, and other sources.

souk (SOOK) – an open-air market or bazaar; from the Arabic word for "marketplace"

sunnah (SOON-nah) – the Muslim guide to righteous living, based on the Koran and on stories of Muhammad's life; from the Arabic word for "way" or "path"

tribute (TRIB-yoot) – a bribe

wadi (WAH-dee) – a river carved by rainy season floods that is dry most of the year

Claire O'Neal has written over two dozen books for Mitchell Lane, including *We Visit Yemen* and *We Visit Iraq*. She holds degrees in English and Biology from Indiana University, and a Ph.D. in Chemistry from the University of Washington. Claire loves to travel, and internationally has visited Great Britain and New Zealand. She lives in Delaware with her husband and two young boys, where she dreams up her next globetrotting adventures.